D0422513

Praise for the Prayers of Malcolm Boyd

"He does not exempt himself in these terse, sometimes slangy, always eloquent prayers; in fact, their eloquence comes from the personal struggle they contain—a struggle to believe, to keep going, a spiritual contest that is agonized, courageous, and not always won."

—*The New York Times*

"This is prayer in the raw, with the last varnish gone—human life, in all its warmth and lovelessness, laid bare before God."

—Bishop John A. T. Robinson, author of *Honest to God*

"Wherever the lonely, the alien, lost, and seeking are, these are Malcolm Boyd's parish."

—*Atlanta Constitution*

"These prayers are vital, extremely contemporary, and have caught on in the ferment of the new cultural revolution."

—*San Francisco Chronicle*

"All will be moved by his pungently expressed compassion. His explicitness and openness are truly tradition-shattering."

—*Library Journal*

"A latter-day Luther or a more worldly Wesley trying to move religion out of 'ghettoized' churches into the streets where the people are."

—*The New York Times Magazine*

Also by Malcolm Boyd

Crisis in Communication

Christ and Celebrity Gods

Focus

If I Go Down to Hell

The Hunger, the Thirst

Are You Running with Me, Jesus?

Free to Live, Free to Die

Malcolm Boyd's Book of Days

The Fantasy Worlds of Peter Stone and Other Fables

As I Live and Breathe: Stages of an Autobiography

My Fellow Americans

Human Like Me, Jesus

The Lover

When in the Course of Human Events (with Paul Conrad)

The Runner

The Alleluia Affair

Christian: Its Meanings in an Age of Future Shock

Am I Running with You, God?

Take Off the Masks

Look Back in Joy

Half Laughing, Half Crying

Gay Priest: An Inner Journey

Edges, Boundaries, and Connections

Rich with Years

Go Gentle into That Good Night

Running with Jesus

The Prayers of Malcolm Boyd

Augsburg

MINNEAPOLIS

*To My Friends, Colleagues, and Mentors
at The Cathedral Center of St. Paul, Los Angeles*

RUNNING WITH JESUS
The Prayers of Malcolm Boyd

Cover design by David Meyer
Book design by Michelle L. Norstad

ISBN 0-8066-4068-5

The paper used in this publication meets the minimum requirements of
American National Standard for Information Sciences—Permanence of
Paper for Printed Library Materials, ANSI Z329.48-1984. ♾ ™

Manufactured in the U.S.A.   AF 9-4068

04   03   02   01   00   1   2   3   4   5   6   7   8   9   10

Contents

Foreword by Martin E. Marty   ix

Introduction   xv
Days and Nights of the Soul   1
Prayers for the Earth, Justice, and Peace   15
Loving and Sexuality   29
In a Retirement Home   39
Prayers on Different Occasions   ·   47
Prayers for Every Day   55
Dilemmas   69
In the City   81
Prayers without Words   91
Jesus Prayers   101

Afterword by Bishop Frederick H. Borsch   109
Afterword by Bishop Paul Wennes Egertson   113

Foreword

Just as he is, without one plea, Malcolm Boyd is standing before Jesus "who bidd'st" him and us to come to him. Despite the title he gave this book and that of a predecessor, Father Boyd is not running all the time. Often he comes across as a lonely contemplative, "tossed about with many a conflict, many a doubt," revealing "fightings and fears within, without. . . ." But now I am depending upon Charlotte Elliott to say in language we find archaic what Boyd has been translating for our years, and what I ought to address in language intending to match his own.

Still, as I read these prayers, I could not help recalling how cries of the heart and words of intention take on classic patterns. Paul, Augustine, Luther, Wesley, or, in Boyd's antecedency, Margery Kempe, William Law, Launcelot Andrewes, Evelyn Underhill, and William Temple did not speak in language borrowed from other times. They had too much on their minds, "just as they were." And all those pray-*ers,* like Boyd, had much to celebrate in response to the One whose "love unknown has broken every barrier down," to use artificial language.

Talk about breaking down barriers: for the four decades I've known him, I've seen Malcolm Boyd in agony and ecstasy trying to see that those barriers remain down. He did it in youth when he had rapport with dissident and restless collegians. He has done it on front lines where people of different races clashed. In the parts of this prayer book that will cause some reviewers and readers to be "dissident and restless," he batters away at sexual barricades set up in the name of texts, traditions, and taboos that, he has argued, need reappraisal in our time. And he has in his seniority served people of his (our) age group, wherein contemporaries die, friendships get tested and need to be cherished afresh, and memories both dim and become enriching. Jesus "bids them" all to follow.

Not long ago I was on a panel with another emeritus scholar who reported that his grandchild had begun a sentence, "Grandpa, now that you're retarded. . . ." At first I winced; mental retardation is not grist for even one cute line. But then I recalled that to "be retarded" means "to be caused to move or proceed slowly; delayed or impeded."

Without question, there is a bit of such retardation evident on these pages. Gone is the young runner's sassy embodiment of WASP chutzpah. But Boyd is wise enough now to see that maturity need not bring a loss of imagination just as it certainly does not mean the end of need for "the Lamb of God" to "receive, welcome, pardon, cleanse, and relieve"—thanks again, Ms. Elliott—anyone who believes the promises.

Right up front, Boyd says he thinks of prayers chiefly as response. Exactly. I've borrowed a life motto from Eugen Rosenstock-Huessy, *respondeo etsi mutabor:* "I respond although I will be changed." This does not mean that *I* am only passive, spiritually comatose, incapable of initiation. But the one who matches "the self-made man, who worships his creator" has less to draw upon, and is less likely to change, than the one who engages in *ressourcement*. This means being called to reach into the resources of the One who calls from the depths, who comes in the Jesus who beckons for response and gets it here in a variety of voices from the pray-er who wrote this book.

What am I doing writing a foreword to a book with so many *I*'s in it? When people give me—another *I*— the chance to speak about worship, I like to say that hymns, prayers, and meditations should take off from the *Te Deum*. They are to be God-focused, theocentric, not merely subjective. One prays more "through" Jesus than "to" Jesus. Yet *Running with Jesus* spends a great deal of energy on the human condition and expends emotion in doing so. How to justify this twist and turn?

The first thing to say is what Father Boyd, who is attentive to things liturgical, would say when conducting worship in Episcopal or other ecumenical contexts: this book is not a template for all prayer, all worship. It has to be seen in complementarity with *Te Deum* and "Praise to the Lord the Almighty." Second, these represent the yang to the yin of divine self-revelation. God reaches in love and needs an object. The praying human reaches back in love and needs the Subject.

Glenn Tinder says that one thing Christians in politics, which means in the polis, in action in the human city must always stay with is "the exalted individual." God honored our species by becoming one of us in the human Jesus here appealed to. That must mean that God cares about the way other humans respond. This is Boyd's way, and some page or other will reach one of us or another in one mood and situation or another.

If you can't get empathic with the author in one or another of his situations, turn the page and let the next prayer catch you. There are plenty of attitudes, moods, and circumstances here to prime your own prayers.

Several years ago Princeton's Donald Capps described many kinds of prayer as a form of constant communication. He modeled it after the conversation between child and parent, something that goes on whether spoken or not. So it is with all prayer and prayers, as this collection teaches us by example. Let us pray.

—Martin E. Marty
Fairfax M. Cone Distinguished Service
Professor Emeritus, University of Chicago

Introduction

My idea of prayer changed when I realized it would no longer be offered to God *up there,* but to God *here;* it was to be natural and real, not phony or contrived; it was not about *other* things—as a rationalized fantasy or escape—but these *things,* however unattractive, jarring, or even socially outcast they might sometimes appear to be.

Prayer, I realized, can be voting, making love, just standing there, being angry, being quiet, cooking spaghetti sauce, marching in a peace or justice demonstration, watering a garden, attending an office meeting, listening, lying on a sick bed, dancing, swimming, starting a new job, walking on a crowded street. Prayer can be filled with color and fun, vitality and pain, hopelessness and starting over again. I like to look out at life as I see it, and pray about it.

An exciting aspect of prayer, for me, is that the old patriarchy is dead. God is not, I discovered, a hierarchical, autocratic, macho "Lord" of a clublike "holy of holies," nor is God an impersonal machine computing sins in a celestial corporate office above the clouds. It came to me that God is loving, even vulnerable, in a terribly unsentimental and profound way, demonstrating the depth, complexity, and holy simplicity of an extraordinary relationship with people.

I came to understand that many prayers are uttered or felt without prescribed forms of piety, sometimes in language imagery that censors might label as profane. If you listen, you can hear sacred thoughts and reflections in the novels, songs, plays, and films of a wide range of contemporary artists. Authentic prayer bridges a heretical gulf between the sacred and secular, the holy and profane. Of course, to hear some genuine prayers, verbal or nonverbal, you must sense what is *not* said.

In 1965, a book of prayers I wrote was published. Langston Hughes called them, simply, poems. The book emerged in silence, with virtually no attention given it. Although *Time* published three of the prayers, it made no comment about them.

Then, five months after publication, *The New York Times* ran a major review praising the book. Soon, nearly everybody was reviewing it. *Are You Running with Me, Jesus?* became a national best-seller with one million copies in print. As the title became familiar, an outpouring of affection for the book took the form of thousands of letters from readers. Its name even began to appear on banners in peace demonstrations. U.S. Senator (and presidential aspirant) Eugene J. McCarthy referred to the book's title in a poem in *The New Republic*. He went on to describe himself as an "existential runner."

What had happened? The spirit of the times had a lot to do with the book's growing reception. There was excitement and a positive thrust in religion that could not be separated from a comparable secular mood, with its Peace Corps imagery of hope, the civil rights struggle, a strong public consciousness of a potential to effect significant changes in society, and a near universal yearning for peace.

I wrote most of the book during the summer and fall of 1964 in Detroit, where I lived in the inner city. The meditation that begins, "Look up at that old window where the old guy is sitting," was based, for example, on a street scene just five blocks from my lodgings near Wayne State University, where I was a chaplain. "The old house is nearly all torn down, Jesus," was a view directly across the street. "The kids are smiling, Jesus, on the tenement stoop" was six blocks away.

The impulse to write the book sprang from my increasing inability to pray. I had always assumed that prayer was necessarily verbal. I forced myself to use the archaic language of liturgical prayer, battling my growing disillusionment and boredom. Wasn't God supposed to be *up there?* When this neat system collapsed for me. I virtually stopped praying, except for using the Lord's Prayer.

In the spring of 1964, a group of Roman Catholic laity and clergy invited me to visit Israel and Rome with them. At one point in the trip we visited the island of Cyprus for a day or so; afterward we proceeded by ship to Haifa. On Cyprus, the men lived dormitory-style in a hostel. One afternoon everybody was taking a nap, despite the sounds of distant gunfire being exchanged by Greek and Turkish Cypriots.

I lay on my cot trying to pray. Then I picked up a ballpoint pen and a notebook. "It's morning, Jesus," I wrote, "and here's that light and sound all over again." The time of day was wrong, but I wasn't being literalistic.

The book was begun. Of course, I didn't know it at the time. I had no idea of writing a book at all. I was grappling with prayer and meditation, trying to get started in a new way. After the tour, I put my notes aside. But that summer I again started thinking about and writing my sacred thoughts.

I sent the book to an editor who was a friend of mine. The publisher for whom he worked accepted it, and the original contract formally titled the book *Prayers for a Post-Christian Era*. The editor explained we would have to move very carefully if I wished the book to be called *Are You Running with Me, Jesus?* The publisher was less than enthusiastic about that proposal. Finally, the editor won approval of my title— but only because the publisher thought the book was doomed to peak at a mere four thousand sales. Thus, what difference could it make *what* the book was called?

Incredible letters I received from readers were the first indication something exciting was happening to *Are You Running with Me, Jesus?* The communications filled pages, dealt with complex matters, were moving. But one terse message remains my favorite: "My sister and I are too old to run with Jesus as we used to," a woman wrote. "Now we're only able to walk with him. Jesus has taken us over some rough terrain but he stayed with us. Old and weary though we are, we can say there is no other way. His hand is large and secure, isn't it?"

The avalanche of letters informed me also that my own life was about to change in ways unknown to me. "Your thoughts, your highs and lows, are familiar to us all," one early reader wrote. An image of the author was being created. I could only stand back and watch in sometime bewilderment and wonder.

Since that time I have written a number of new prayers, many of which can be found in these pages. A second volume, *Human Like Me, Jesus,* appeared. And numerous prayers have been written for special occasions (one was for the dedication of a new cathedral) and for urgent needs (the AIDS crisis, for example, and the incurable illness of the young daughter of a friend).

Prayer, I've learned, is more my response to God than a matter of my own initiative. I believe Jesus Christ prays *in* me as well as *for* me. But my response—like the psalmist's—is sporadic, moody, now despairing, now joyful, corrupted by my self-interest and frequent desire to manipulate God's love. The widespread, often hidden, community that is open to the Spirit of God incarnates prayer in its essential life. My own prayer is a part of this.

Now we find ourselves in a new, complex, and challenging century, with many deep changes in our life and world. Yet Jesus remains our closest companion, our savior who shares living and dying with us.

I invite you to share this book's spiritual journey with me.

Days and Nights of the Soul

It's morning, Jesus. It's morning, and here's that light and sound all over again. I've got to move fast . . . get into the bathroom, wash up, grab a bite to eat, and run some more.

I just don't feel like it. What I really want to do is get back into bed, pull up the covers, and sleep. All I seem to want today is the big sleep, and here I've got to run all over again.

Where am I running? You know I can't understand these things. It's not that I need to have you tell me. What counts most is just that somebody knows, and it's you. That helps a lot.

So I'll follow along, okay? But lead, please. Now I've got to run. Are you running with me, Jesus?

I'm crying and shouting inside tonight, Jesus, and I'm feeling completely alone. All the roots I thought I had are gone. Everything in my life is in an upheaval. I am amazed that I can maintain any composure when I'm feeling like this.

The moment is all that matters; the present moment is of supreme importance. I know this. Yet in the present I feel dead. I want to anchor myself in the past and shed tears of self-pity. When I look ahead tonight I can see only futility, pain, and death. I am only a rotting body, a vessel of disease, potentially a handful of ashes after I am burned.

But you call me tonight to love and responsibility. You have a job for me to do. You make me look at other persons whose needs make my self-pity a mockery and a disgrace.

Jesus, I hear you. I know you. I feel your presence strongly in this awful moment, and I thank you. Help me onto my feet. Help me to get up.

I'm nowhere, and I couldn't care less. It's so still. Am I on the moon? Am I on the earth? Am I *here* at all? But, if so, where?

I feel disengaged from life at this moment. Time has stopped, and nothing matters. I have nowhere to hurry, no place to go, no sensible goal. I might as well be dead.

I want to feel a breeze blow against my face, or the hot sun warming me. I want to feel life, Jesus. Help me to feel love or anger or laughter. Help me to care about life again.

I'm scared, Jesus. You've asked me to do something I don't think I can do. I'm sure I wouldn't want to do it except that you asked me.

But I don't feel strong enough, and you know I lack the courage I'd need. Why did you ask me to do this? It seems to me that Jim could do this much, much more easily. Remember, I told you I'm afraid to stand up and be criticized, Jesus. I feel naked in front of everybody, and I can't hide any part of myself.

Why can't I be quiet and have peace and be left alone? I don't see what good it will do for me to be dragged out in front of everybody and do this for you. Don't misunderstand me. I'm not saying I won't do it. I'm just saying I don't *want* to do it. I mean, how in the hell *can* I do it?

You know me better than anybody does, but then you go and ask me to do something crazy like this. I can't figure you out. I wish you'd just leave me alone today, but if this is what you think is best, I'll try. I'll try. But I don't want to. Pray for me, Jesus.

I know it sounds corny, Jesus, but I'm lonely. I wasn't going to get lonely anymore, and so I kept very busy, telling myself I was serving you. But it's getting dark again, and I'm alone; honestly, Christ, I'm lonely as hell.

Why do I feel so sorry for myself? There's no reason why I should be. You're with me, and I know it. I'll be with other people in a little while. I know some of them love me very much in their own way, and I love some of them very much in mine.

But I still feel so damned lonely right now, in this minute that I'm living. I feel confused about how to get through the next few hours. It's silly, but I feel this way because I'm threatened by me, and I wish I could get through to you, clearly and with a kind of purity and integrity.

And yet, while I say this to you, I've been unkind to certain people whom you also love, and I've added to misunderstanding and confusion.

Take hold of me and connect me with other people, Jesus. Give me patience and love so that I can listen when I plug into these other lives. Help me to listen and listen and listen . . . and love by being quiet and serving, and being there.

You said there is perfect freedom in your service, Jesus. Well, I don't feel perfectly free. I don't feel free at all. I'm a captive to myself.

I do what I want. I have it all my own way. There is no freedom at all for me in this, Jesus. Today I feel like a slave bound in chains and branded by a hot iron because I'm a captive to my own will and don't give an honest damn about you or your will.

You're over there where I'm keeping you, outside my real life. How can I go on being such a lousy hypocrite? Come over here, where I don't want you to come. Let me quit playing this blasphemous game of religion with you. Help me to let you be yourself in my life—so that I can be myself.

The drinks are tranquilizing me. But even while I'm being tranquilized, I don't want to be.

I remember the cutting edge you lived on. You didn't get tranquilized. You went right on, and then you gave back love. I seem to have run out of love, and I'm relating very badly right now.

Don't leave me alone, Christ, because I've left you. I just want the easy way out, any way out at all, but you know I really don't. I hurt inside and wish I could tear myself away.

Get me back on my own cutting edge. Help me to put away the tranquilizers and just be myself with you and the others you place with me.

I'm having a great day, and I just want to thank you, Jesus. Yesterday I was down, but today I'm up again. These people I'm with are loving and supportive. The sun has really come out for me. I see everything in bright reds and yellows.

I hated the dark reds and the crying blues yesterday. I was mean, Christ, and vicious, and I can hardly understand how anybody put up with me. But they didn't beat me down. They let me know what it is to be human because *they* stayed human. Now I'm human again. I feel good, and I want to get out with people and connect with them.

There's somebody I was mean to yesterday. I want to knock myself out to be nice to him today. Honestly, Jesus, thank you.

I want to be alone and not to be alone, both at the same time. I can't stand anybody being around at this moment. The sound of another voice seems to cut into my aching flesh. I want to be alone. I crave silence, even a vacuum, an endless echo chamber of silence upon silence upon silence. Cold. Alone. Silence.

But this silence is filled with demons, so that I'm not alone at all. I'm with demons. And I'd rather be with other people, Jesus, and with you. I've thought it out, and this is what I want. Will you help me cut loose from these demons so I can be with you and the other people?

I feel so cold, and I want to warm myself by a fire. Please give me the fire to thaw out the icy coldness inside me. Warm me, Jesus, so I can give out some real warmth to some other very cold people.

The blood ran to my head, Jesus, and I almost flipped. I was mad and couldn't think clearly. Thanks for cooling me down.

If I'd been on my own, I would have done something bad to somebody whom you love just as much as me. I was very vulnerable, Jesus, and he didn't realize he'd hit me in a spot so soft I should put up a neon sign over it that flashes "danger" twenty-four hours a day.

He hit, and I screamed inside, which is the worst kind of screaming. Then the heat flashed, and I couldn't make sense and just wanted revenge. I wanted to hurt him, Jesus.

But you spoke to me. I heard you. Afterward, I was still sitting there, and he was still sitting there. I knew I was okay, that I hadn't done anything that would really louse everybody up.

Thank you for being there with me and cooling me down. Thanks for taking hold of me.

It's bumper to bumper, and the traffic is stalled. My radio is on, and I'm listening to the news again. In a few minutes, there will be some more music.

I want to get home, Jesus, but the traffic won't move. I'm tired from working, tired of waiting, tired of listening to the stupid radio. I'm too damned tired to be patient, and I'm hot and sweaty. I've worked hard all day, and I want to get home. I don't feel like being loving or patient or kind or long-suffering. Not right now. Later, maybe.

If I could have anything in the world right now, it would be a road stretching out ahead, empty, all other cars gone, and a beautiful freeway for miles and miles, just for me, and then *home*. I've just about had it today. Really, it's too much. Don't ask me to be patient.

Okay, I'll try some more to be human, but it's nearly been knocked out of me for one day. Stay with me; I can't do it alone.

Jesus, thanks for sweating it out with me here on this highway.

I'm exhausted, Jesus, but sleep won't come. My brain keeps whirring with thoughts, and it won't turn off. I have to get up early in the morning, and I'm desperate for a good night's rest. I can't get cool. I keep telling myself to quiet down and drop off, but it just won't work.

I keep rotating, Jesus, first on my stomach, then on my back, then on my side, and on my other side, and on my stomach again. I can't lie still.

The night is going to slip away and pretty soon the light will come, and I'll be dead tired. I'm worried, and I can't let go. So many things on my mind. What's going to happen, Jesus? What's going to happen? Help me to stop asking. Turn me off.

Bless my sleep. Let me sleep. Help me to sleep. And then wake me up when the light comes, will you? Please wake me up, and let me be refreshed in your strength.

Jesus, it's evening again. What happened to this day? I'm not sure I found you in it, as it was moving and I was moving, too. I'm not at all clear whether I loved people today or got involved in life in the way I know you wanted me to do. Maybe I just kept life moving along. But, if so, *why?*

Now I'm too tired to think about it rationally. Tomorrow is coming close: Will it be the same? But, if so, *why?*

I become frightened, Jesus, as the day ends and I feel my life being spent, and my human time draining away. I feel so small in an age of science and space. These are hard moments when I cry and wonder what meaning I can find in the midst of complexity and rapid change. Help me to understand what it means for you to be the creator and sovereign of science, space, this city, and the whole of life. And, of this evening, even with its shadows and fears, and all its love and promise.

I'm grateful things broke this way. I didn't know quite what to do before. Nothing would give at all. Nothing would give an inch. Everything was stymied and, Jesus, I was, too.

Everything had been gray for so long. Nothing was going my way at all, and I felt so permanently lousy.

Thanks, Jesus, for the sun coming out. Thanks for this real break and for making me feel alive again.

Prayers for the Earth,
Justice, and Peace

I see black and white, Jesus. I see white teeth in a black face.

I see black eyes in a white face.

Help us to see *persons*, Jesus—not a black person or a white person or a brown person, but human persons.

What was Hiroshima like, Jesus, when the bomb fell? What went through the minds of mothers, what happened to the lives of children, what stabbed at the hearts of men when they were caught up in a sea of flame?

What was Auschwitz like, Jesus, when the crematoriums belched the stinking smoke from the burned bodies of people? When families were separated, the weak perished, the strong faced inhuman tortures of the spirit and the body. What was the concentration camp like, Jesus?

Tell us, Christ, that we, living now, are capable of the same cruelty, the same horror, if we turn our back on you, our brother, and our sisters and brothers. Save us from ourselves; spare us the evil of our hearts' good intentions, unbridled and mad. Turn us from our perversions of love, especially when these are perpetrated in your name. Speak to us about war, and about peace, and about the possibilities for both in our very human hearts.

We know you love the world that you created and redeemed. We who stand in the world offer ourselves and our society for your blessing and healing.

We confess that we have failed to love as you did. We have been socially unjust, and our society is imperfect, fragmented, and sometimes sick to death.

Teach us your ways in the world and in this life that we share together. Don't let us restrict you to a narrow ghetto labeled "religion," but lead us to worship you in the fullness of life.

Give us light to seek true morality in sacrifice and open responsibility, not in narrow legalisms. Show us how to express our love for you in very specific, human service to other people.

Jesus, change our hearts from hearts of stone to hearts of flesh, and let us give thanks to you for all of life.

How may the heart be taught, Jesus? When a mind is closed and communication has ceased, how may a person be reached? If one's heart has never learned to love, or has stopped loving, how may the heart be taught, Jesus?

Why can't we permit the liberation of people and living things, Jesus? Why can't we permit our own liberation?

"The universe has consciousness," the young Latino told me. "But the world is now uninhabitable. People are acting fiercely against the consciousness of the universe."

It seems to me we have a deadly definition of gods. We feel that to be a god is to ride roughshod over the earth, make decisions capriciously, act without feeling, and try to create terror in other people. We feel that to be a god is to claim the whole earth, and all of life within it, for our own use and destruction.

Can we start acting like humans, Jesus?

Somebody forgot to push the right button, Jesus. So all hell broke loose. Airline schedules are loused up, somebody is shouting at somebody else who can't help the situation, a lot of money has been lost, and about two dozen people are caught up in a cybernetic tangle. We've missed our plane, which isn't our fault, and I was due in Chicago to participate in a meeting forty-five minutes ago.

Please cool everybody off, including me, because I'm one of the people involved, and I'm hot right now and shouting angrily at someone else who can't help the cybernetic crisis any more than I can.

And, Jesus, please keep us human and capable of weathering such minor—and major—disasters. Don't let us turn ourselves into machines, no matter how hard we seem to be trying.

Maria has AIDS and is dying, Jesus. She worries a lot about what will happen to her kids when she dies. Maria has had a long struggle and fought courageously. What disturbs me most is that I feel her death isn't really necessary, Jesus. If there had been more public awareness when AIDS began, if money had been poured into research, if politicians had quit playing it safe with prejudice and treated AIDS as the health crisis it is, thousands of deaths like Maria's might have been prevented. How can I forgive this deathly and public sin, Jesus?

Can more lives be saved now, Jesus, if we wake up and exert full energy to defeat AIDS?

Please *wake* us up, Jesus.

She doesn't feel like an animal, Jesus, even though she's being treated like one. She looks sixty but she isn't yet forty years old. She is a migrant farm worker. She's been working in this field all day—and day here means sunrise to sunset. Afterward, she'll go back with her family to spend the night in a one-room tin shack most people wouldn't let their dog live in.

Nothing seems to be gained by her suffering and deprivation, Jesus. She never gets ahead financially. The small amount of money taken in is already owed for groceries. She needs medical care she'll never receive. Her husband is just as much a beast of burden as she. Their children seem already to be caught in the same vicious circle of exploitation.

There is still a vision of humanness inside her mind and soul, Jesus, although her body is broken and her face is wasted. Should she nourish any glimmer of hope, or would it be better for her to erase hope from her consciousness? What happens to a society that takes such a toll on human life and doesn't care?

I've searched for community in many places, Jesus. I was often looking in the wrong places, but I don't think my motive was altogether wrong. I was looking futilely and without much hope for belonging and acceptance.

Now in this moment I'm here with these others for only a few hours. I will be gone tomorrow. However, I realize I have found community where and as it is. I acknowledge it gratefully as your gift.

I won't be searching so desperately anymore, because I know that I must accept community wherever you offer it to me. I accept it in this moment. Thank you, Jesus.

She hadn't meant to let drugs take over her life. At first it was just a thrill, a sensation; part of a longing for a sense of deeper awareness; fitting in as a part of her small circle of friends.

Soon, drugs became necessary—so she thought. The highs were brief, oh so brief, but demanding. The lows, unbearable—Irene scarcely functioned. It occurred to her: She *had* to get high again.

But she lost track of herself—who she was. Her marriage ended bitterly, her former husband taking custody of the kids. Her job—it was a great one, she had worked for years to get it and was ideally suited for it—disappeared amid embarrassment, despair, and guilt.

Friends drew away, for she began to move in an underside of life. Irene was obsessed, in thrall, destroying even the last vestige of what she perceived to be her true self.

Be with her in her treatment to get well, Christ. Guide her. Give her wisdom and strength for the struggle to live.

Three young children died in that room. It's just a room in a slum, in a big American city. But when a fire started it became a very special room, a death chamber for three youngsters.

They tell me eleven people have died in this area of a few blocks, Jesus. All died in fires when they were trapped and couldn't get out. The people in the area can't move away because there's no place for them to go.

It doesn't seem fair that some people have nice homes with safety, Christ, while other people can't get out of a slum like this except in a coffin.

What can I do about war and peace? How can I do anything that will affect the power structures that hold the key to basic decisions about waging war or maintaining peace? I've marched in peace demonstrations, fasted in protest against nuclear experiments, signed petitions, and tried seriously to study the issues involved. But what have I been able to accomplish?

It's painfully frustrating trying to bring about meaningful changes while being confronted by solid resistance.

I see the beauty of your creation and am grateful, but then I see in my mind's eye the very real possibility of its destruction. How can I stand this, Jesus? What is prayer supposed to mean if I am passively accepting a peril, which it is sinful to accept? I don't want to misuse prayer to lull me about this crisis, Jesus. I want to accept my responsibility of cooperating with you in the continuing and present act of creation. How can I do that?

It takes away my guilt when I blame your murder on the Jews, Jesus. Why should I feel guilty about it? I wasn't there. If I had been, I can't imagine myself shouting anything about crucifying you.

The Roman soldiers were there, of course, along with Pontius Pilate. And the Jews were there, the Sanhedrin and those who cried for Barabbas instead of you.

I wasn't there, Jesus. I had nothing to do with it.

I *was* there, Jesus, as you know. I am a part of humanness, although I like to remember it only when I want something from my sister or brother or society at large, and I like to forget it when it involves me in life outside myself.

I shouted for your crucifixion, Jesus. I taunted you as you bore your cross, and I stood in the crowd to watch you die.

I did this again, just today, Jesus.

Forgive me. I ask for your mercy and forgiveness. But how can I ask forgiveness of Jews, after the pogroms, burnings, genocide, every form of discrimination, and most of it in your name? In your own humanity, you were a Jew. I am involved in your murder, Jesus, as in the lives and deaths of countless Jews.

I ask forgiveness of you for the guilt I share in the deaths of Jews murdered by Christians in your name, for the guilt I share in the countless persecutions of Jews by Christians in your name.

I am shamed. I am mute.

We can't make it alone, Jesus. God knows, we've tried, and we've even reached the point where we could blow up everybody, including ourselves. Teach us how to listen carefully and patiently to other people. Teach us how to say what we have to say clearly, simply, and openly. Teach us what responsibility toward you and others really means.

Cut through all our egoism and self-interest, Jesus. Make us understand what patriotism must mean in one world of conflicting nationalisms. Educate us to support community wherever it brings people together in a shared sense of human concern. Work with us, Christ, to bridge gulfs and divisions between nations and persons.

My body and the planet Earth are closely connected, Jesus. Hiking on a mountain pass, I see the lacework intricacy of your creation in the trees, leaves, foliage, stones, flowers, dirt, mud, glimpses of the sky above, and the sounds of birds singing near me.

Walking in the early morning on a beach, I share it with a distant figure holding a fishing pole. The energy of the ocean leaps out at me in the mystery of its waves and the earthy, roaring sound coming from the deep within its being. Standing here, I am grateful for the harmony of life that is your creation. The beach is my church, and I give thanks for the existence of ultimate goodness in your spirit.

I take watchful care of my body, as you know. I exercise, eat foods that are nutritious, deal creatively with stress whenever I can, and realize I am the steward of my body.

But what can I do to maintain the health of the planet Earth? I see clearly that human greed endangers it. Its oceans and rivers are polluted, its ozone layer depleted, forests and wildlife are threatened, resources laid waste by developers and exploiters. Its cities, including mine, are being strangled.

The planet Earth is where you lived and died, isn't it, Jesus? Your thirty-three years were spent on its soil. You ate its bread and fruit and fish, drank its water and wine. You knew and loved its people, strode along a quiet beach under its moon, watched its sun rise and fall, lingered in its wilderness, and climbed its hills.

Awaken us, Jesus, to preserve this planet that we have shared together. Stir up our love and courage to
save the oceans
save the forests
save the farms
save the towns and cities
save the rivers and lakes
save the mountains and hills
save the flowers and trees
save the animals and wildlife
save ourselves.

Loving and Sexuality

This young girl got pregnant, and she isn't mar-
ried. There was this guy, you see, and she had had a little too much to drink. It sounds so stupid, but the
loneliness was real. Where were her parents during all
this? It's hard to know. To the girl, they probably
seemed indifferent, absorbed in their familiar routines,
uninterested in her real life. But did she ever try to tell
them about it? And would they have listened?

Now the guy doesn't want anything to do with her;
he's tied up in some job and is very busy. He's especially annoyed about the idea of the child and wonders
why she didn't know better. He thought she understood what the rules were: A woman doesn't have to
get pregnant these days if she doesn't want to.

The girl is sitting across from me now, so cool and
collected. She can't even admit to herself how hurt she
is, and goes on analyzing the situation with bits of
freshman psychology. And, meanwhile, there's a new
life growing inside her, making new demands on her;
does the textbook have an answer to that?

There's nothing ahead for her with the guy. She tells
me he's really in love with somebody else. She's not in
love with anyone; she's sure of that. And she's honest
enough to admit, even knowing what she does now, that

she'd go back to sleeping with the guy. Does she really think that's all she needs? She admits she's thought of suicide but says she doesn't have the strength to make any real decision, let alone that one.

What am I going to tell her, Jesus? How can I help her understand the nature of the love she's looking for?

Ken and Tom stand before the altar in a church, Jesus. They have decided to throw in their human lot together, to share and love each other—in sickness and health, prosperity and poverty, enthusiasm and despair.

Both had yearned for a shared life, creating a real home with friends, responsibilities, and interests in common. Each looked for another man with whom to share wholeness.

Ken's mother and father are here. Tom's parents, opposed to his being gay and to this service, are absent. A few of their siblings are here. The minister is giving a short homily following music and readings. Ken and Tom will exchange rings and say a few words to each other, expressing their love and what this covenant of commitment means to them.

They hold hands and are smiling.

You share my time and space, my heart, my being. After we make love, you hold me in your arms. My heart pounding, I lie upon your chest. We stay here quietly. My universe is defined by the perimeter of your flesh, consciousness, and soul.

I think of getting up to make two cups of coffee. Shall we read the morning paper, get dressed, go out? But I don't move.

Bless us, Jesus. Bind us close. Let us have more days and years of joy, growth, responsibility, passion, quiet, and trust as your gift.

They've been married for twenty years, Jesus, and they say they hate each other. They want a divorce— that's the one thing they're sure of. Not that either of them is in love with anyone else. There just doesn't seem to be much love in the whole situation. Was it simply sex that brought them together, and sex that is killing them now?

They keep accusing each other of long-standing infi- delities and tell you they would have broken up long ago except for the children, but the children seem merely weapons to be used against each other. And then, when they've finally decided—once again—to make a real break, they end up in bed together at 4 A.M., and everything is fine until the next evening, when they feel it's time for a final break again.

They've hurt each other so terribly; no marriage counselor can undo what they've worked at so long. They've been to the psychiatrist and the minister and anyone else who would listen, with or without being paid for it, but no one knows how hate and love get so mixed up with each other. Or wasn't there any love here, Christ, ever?

Where do sex and love come together in these two lives? Should they try to make it alone or together? Can they make it together, Jesus? Can they make it alone?

She meets him at her apartment when he lies to his wife about why he's not home. What does she expect from this brief encounter? She experiences a searing, sweet, romantic sensation with a time limit. She expresses a naked, hungry need to pour out her unfulfilled life. Yet he has told her he is happily married and does not intend to leave his wife.

She wonders, more and more, what it means to "make love." The good-byes she has to say, and accept, are cool and brittle. She asks herself if the final one won't be a tersely bitten-off end that seems to jab like a needle seeking blood.

How much hurt can she stand? Will she come to understand what a full sexual union involves in terms of human relationship?

They share stories at the end of a stressful, work-filled day, Jesus. They hear about their respective days: relating to people, different situations and scenarios, sometime crises. This is brief but valuable time when the day's luggage is put away. It becomes a moment of communion.

The passing years have been kind to them. When they disagree or fall victim to anxieties or anger, they share their moods and hurts. They manage to stay sensitive to each other's feelings and their own.

Bless them, Jesus, in their love of each other and of you.

They have been in love for forty years, Jesus. They will be the first to say it wasn't all a bed of roses. They accepted their relationship as the primary fact in their lives, so they simply spent more time and energy on it than on anything else.

However, they avoided giving it excess energy. Very wisely, they sought intellectual and cultural involvement with a number of other people, often separately. They acknowledged the spiritual side of themselves and allowed it to develop patiently.

Humor has helped a lot. And the discipline of getting on with life in place of wondering whether they ought to or not. Listening as well as speaking. An unrelenting awareness of how stiflingly boring boredom can be.

She is serene in the world and with her lover. At first, her marriage to Christopher was a happy experience. Motherhood followed. They had three children together. After a long time the realization came that she was not fulfilled as Christopher's wife.

But why? There was no other man who attracted her. When she met Dorothy, the truth leapt at her irresistibly. Yet she found difficulty initially in accepting herself as a lesbian. Hadn't she known herself through all the previous years?

The love she felt for Dorothy was overwhelming and satisfying. It became the greatest challenge of her life to change her primary relationship with grace and a minimum of hurt and misunderstanding. Christopher was aware theirs had long been an unrewarding relationship, and he acceded to her wishes for a divorce. The children, out of college and into their own careers and relationships, understood.

She and Dorothy settled into their new life as partners and lovers, this at an age when many people turn away from risk. These two women are actively loving in a human, spiritual, and sexual relationship.

They ask for your blessing, Jesus.

The seasons of their love move more rapidly. How did winter arrive so suddenly with a burst of cold and sleet? The world seems more deliberately shut out now. Their home is intimate and warm, its mood quieter.

Spring played games: Would it ever come? Then it did. It bears them along as if it were a fast-moving stream. They are happy to be alive, eager for what is fresh.

In summer they spend most of their time out of doors, making a patio into another room, working later in their garden. It is a time for flowers, a bluebird, and even a hummingbird that visits.

Autumn sweeps in with a rush of wind. Yellow and red leaves fall to the ground. Wood is gathered for burning in the hearth. Autumn is a time of anticipation, changes to come, and an awareness of the mystery of life.

Your seasons are gifts of grace, Jesus.

In a Retirement Home

"Go away," she says almost inaudibly, forming the words precisely with her lips. Her eyes are hard.

I try to joke, play with her, soften this moment. It is part of my regular visit to her retirement home. Always in the past she held my hand, spoke to me earnestly with her eyes, entreated me not to leave.

Trying to effect a change in her depressed mood, I move my fingers in a playful way as if I were making dancing figures of them against a wall. I talk to her and laugh.

"You're crazy," she announces, giving me an uncompromising look of dismissal. "Go away," she repeats slowly. "Don't come back."

I feel frustrated and defeated; I cannot imagine what has prompted her anger and rejection. A few moments later, a nurse speaks to me outside her room. "She's feeling pretty low today. She's always very unhappy when her daughter stays away a long time and doesn't come to see her."

Patience and understanding. They are needed, especially in a retirement home, aren't they, Jesus?

"I want to die," she whispered. That was during my last visit. Now the TV set is turned on loud, characters in a soap opera talk, and she doesn't see or hear them because she is asleep.

She's snoring, her head laid back on a pillow in the chair she occupies when she isn't confined to her bed.

She is over ninety years old. Loved by members of her family, she asked to be placed in a retirement home because she felt life would be easier for her here. Nonetheless, now she finds living itself an insuperable burden and would like to be released from any more of it.

Suddenly she awakens. She remembers an old prayer in German from her youth and starts to recite it. "A pillow," she whispers. "Please bring a pillow for my back." I talk to her for a while. She nods and smiles, occasionally utters a few words in German.

I kiss her forehead and say good-bye.

She is still a beautiful woman in her eighties. Always, she shows me what seems to be a genuinely motivated smile when she greets me. And she invariably wears a neat, good-looking dress and selected pieces of jewelry. A stylish hat sits next to her on her bed.

A photograph of her late husband is on her dresser. When she speaks of him, she cries softly. "I loved him so. I miss him. Why did he have to leave me alone?" But in a moment she has regained her composure.

On another visit, I find her holding a newspaper. "These poor homeless people on the street," she exclaims. "Isn't it awful?" Tears stream from her eyes, down her cheeks.

We say the Lord's Prayer together while we hold hands. She says the words firmly and loudly, her eyes opened, her head unbowed.

"It's good of you to come to visit me," she says, smiling. I see her as youthful, always getting ready to go out and confront life optimistically, expecting what is good and true to happen to her.

The fact that she could die so soon eluded me. On my recent visits I had noticed she was very frail, unsure, and her eyesight was failing rapidly. Yet her basic good humor was so intact, she fooled me.

The last time I saw her we were not alone. Her granddaughter, a college student, visited also. This provided an entirely different focus than usual for our conversation. There was a bright cheer to the occasion. Boisterous laughter replaced the sober note of previous visits when her problems were discussed, even though kept beneath a veneer of polite control.

So today I was unprepared, when I sought her out, to find she died last Tuesday. I suppose she died as she seemed to live: buoyant, smiling softly, taking simply another small step instead of a plunge.

I used to be afraid of her. Because she is totally blind and nearly deaf, she would jump when I drew close, reacting like a frightened bird. I didn't know how to calm her.

But then I learned simply to hold her two hands in one of mine, and place my other hand on her shoulder. This reassured her, provided her a necessary security.

"Who are you?" she asks me each time, in exactly the same voice.

"I'm the man who comes to pray with you," I reply.

"*Oh*, how *nice,*" she says, brightening.

We talk. She tells me sometimes that she used to give young students piano lessons. So, she explains, she is a very precise, disciplined person, one who wants to wrest exact meanings from words. After we say the Lord's Prayer, she explains that "thy will be done, *in earth* as it is in heaven," is preferable, in her opinion, to "*on earth.*"

When I bring her Holy Communion, she asks, "What is it?"

"The bread of heaven," I reply.

"*Oh*, how *nice,*" she says. Our ritual never varies. She accepts a sacramental wafer in her mouth.

Now her face lights. She holds my hands in one of

hers, and with her other hand she traces the lines below my eyes and on my forehead.

"The bread of heaven," she repeats quietly. We sit together without words, no longer afraid of each other.

"One of my sons just had his seventieth birthday," **she says.** She is ninety-five, delicate as a bird, yet an incredibly tough survivor. A while back she fell and broke her hip, but she has recovered. Shingles come and go, visiting her face and head.

Her hair is neatly brushed this morning. She uses a cane when she gets up to open the door and greet me. She's wiry, energetic, agile.

Most remarkable, in my view, is how my visits to her ironically help *me*. Her sense of humor is strongly intact. Deeper than that, however, is a sturdy structure of faith, well-being, and an indestructible awareness of the continuity of life.

She is like an old tree whose roots penetrate into the earth. She has long weathered storms and years. Now she simply awaits the next season, whatever storm or peace may come.

Prayers on Different Occasions

I've got to get into the left lane now, Jesus. All the energy of my life is suddenly focused on this sole objective. For the past few seconds my left turn signal has been blinking, but no one has let me into the lane on this crowded highway. Now the intersection where I must turn is only a few feet away.

Cars speed past. A sense of panic seizes me. Perhaps I'm somehow out of place here and can't compete. Is this such a deadly business as it seems, or do we all know we're playing a child's game? If I can't get into the lane, I'll be quite late. It's madness. The highway doesn't belong to anyone driving on it. Why must I fight for the small space I need, Jesus?

The system has to work. I know that. If it falls apart here, it can't be depended on anywhere. I see inches to spare in front of the speeding car coming up on my left. I swerve over. The car slackens its pace. Now it pulls back, easily and deliberately. I have found a friend.

Mike, my dog, was dying on that rainy day. I had often wondered about the relationship between Mike and the human world. How he had looked at life, houses, shops from a speeding car, lights in tall buildings at night, authority and freedom, the human schedule he had grown accustomed to, squirrels and cats—and me.

Mike, who was sixteen years old, struggled to stand up. I reached out to touch the head and body of my close companion before he died.

Thank you for the mystery, the simplicity and wonder, of the relationship between Mike and me, Jesus.

A frame separates me from a face in a picture. I'm standing here in a museum gallery, looking at it. It seems to me that the person painted in oils inside the frame wishes to communicate, maybe share a word or a feeling, and somehow relate to me. I hate to deny the urgency of this moment by simply walking away.

I want to throw away all frames, Jesus.

I went with some children to the zoo yesterday. It was a nice morning; the wind was brisk, the sun shining. The children had old friends to call upon, so I followed along. First we saw the rhinoceros. There were some rhinoceros babies, too, and all of us exchanged greetings with them. Next we went to see the hippopotamus family. Everybody looked at everybody else for a while, some of us outside cages, others inside. There seemed to be a sense of mutual liking and acceptance.

Then we visited the walrus. It was an incredible ham, zooming through the water on its back, turning hand flips, coming up for fish and applause, suddenly disappearing beneath dramatically turbulent waves. I could identify easily with the walrus, for I have often fantasized such behavior in my own bathtub.

Thanks for the zoo, Jesus.

I am seated inside a theater. In my anonymity, I feel shut off from every distraction. The screen is remote, *up there,* and I'm down here, able to relate or not relate to it.

The film has begun. It is telling a story. It involves people. Now I recognize myself. I'm up there, too, Jesus, trying to make a decision. It's painful and I'm suffering. Yet I feel the closeness of other persons near me in the theater. I'm not suffering alone.

We are so naked, Jesus, sitting here together and seeing ourselves (and each other) up there. Only the story isn't *up there* anymore. It's *here*.

When the movie has ended, and the lights come up, will we remember our closeness, or will we all be quite alone? At first I wanted both escape and communion inside this theater. Now I know I can't escape, Jesus, and also how much I need communion.

I saw the man on the moon. His face looked very full when I was a kid. He wore a grin of sorts. I considered him benign, a little foolish, certainly harmless. Why he was up there, I had no idea. But I used to look at him and wonder.

Later I heard the face wasn't a face at all, only canals and rivers and mountains making a pattern. I was sorry to lose the human touch up in the sky with the stars at night, but frankly I didn't worry about it. Finally, when astronauts went into space and landed on the moon, I saw them walking around.

What new surprises await me in space, Jesus? Help me to get ready for them and to understand.

Today she is seventy years old, Jesus. Everybody else is concerned about her birthday celebration while she is cooking breakfast and planning a visit to the grocery store.

It doesn't seem possible to her that she is seventy. Where did the years go? Her interests and thoughts are very young ones, moving backward swiftly over many years.

Where did the last week go so quickly? The last day—the last hour? Time is running through a sieve.

But, of course, she is not bound by it. She is free. Fear is merely a word. She sees her mother and father. Remember the picnic when she turned ten years old? She sees her college roommate and her Latin teacher and her husband and her baby and. . . .

Someone is telephoning to wish her a happy birthday.

She doesn't understand why nobody seems to realize how young she really is, Jesus.

Christmas Eve. Outside the window the afternoon light is fading. I'll sit here in the quiet for a few moments before I light the Christmas tree, turn on a lamp.

Other Christmas Eves crowd into my mind. How can I understand Christmas Eve, Jesus, beneath the tinsel and music, wrapping of presents, and pictures everywhere of you as a baby in a manger?

These next few hours—will I simply feel emptiness and longing? Try to cover them up with laughter and bright lights? But I want to feel the deep meaning of this night.

Tell me, what was Christmas Eve like?

Prayers for Every Day

I cut up onions, garlic, and mushrooms, and place them in a large pan on the stove. My spaghetti sauce is under way. It's restful to cook when I don't feel the pressure of a deadline. I just putter, pouring oregano and basil as if I were an alchemist, stir the ingredients, add meat, fresh tomatoes, and tomato sauce. Grated cheese stands ready.

The simmering mix seems to make a nurturing and comfortable sound in the quiet kitchen. The stove is transformed into a holy altar of life. What I am cooking is not a work of art that will claim a lasting place or excite human admiration for long. One of life's small pleasures, it will be gobbled up gratefully and forgotten.

Yet this is a special task for me. It's unselfish compared to many things I do; truly an offering to a few friends. It's meticulous work; a right or wrong decision can be crucial. I reach for the tarragon.

I find it a sacred time of kitchen meditation to stir, smell, add, taste, grate, ponder, and let simmer.

The time has come to move that picture on the wall. It's important, I decide, to do new things, take risks. Everything has been too settled around here for a long time. But where shall I place it?

Over *there* near the bookcase. Only that means I'll have to move the bookcase and the couch and that table and the plants. It's worth it. The room will look much better, have a fresh ambiance.

I move the bookcase and the couch and that table and the plants. I place the picture in its new location. I like it.

However, I have no idea what to put on the wall in the spot where the picture used to hang. The empty space mocks me, ridicules my impulsive ingenuity.

It's easier to leave everything where it already belongs, not to change or move a picture, isn't it? But I mustn't settle for this, Jesus. I don't want to. Help me to take risks.

I water the garden. It is a good feeling of companionship with the earth to help it sustain life.

I soak the dry grass, make a special effort to revitalize a bougainvillea plant that is sick, and spray expectant pansies lightly so that I will not bruise them.

The plant over in the corner that is hard to reach was ailing but seems to be doing well now. A huge, healthy bush needs to be pruned soon. Small plants in a big pot await my attention.

It's lovely here. Wind chimes sing out in a cool breeze. I marvel at the patience of the plants and flowers. The gentle way they respond to love is touching. Can I learn?

Housecleaning is a ritual. Open windows! Let in fresh air! Bustle and clean carpets and cushions, mop floors, wash windows, dust, cleanse, sweep!

Housecleaning is good for the soul. It gives one something practical to do. The body and soul are working together. One can see results before one's eyes.

But be sure to get into every cranny and corner with a broom, a brush, a rag. Wipe glass covering pictures hanging on walls. Shake dust. Cleanse counters.

Wash dishes. Take down draperies and curtains. Make tile floors shine.

Doing this, I know instinctively that I must also engage myself soon in a seasonal housecleaning of the soul. Yes. This, without undue delay.

I have a fever. It paralyzes my senses. I don't have the will or strength to get out of bed. I can scarcely turn my body over.

The fever is like an electric current moving behind my eyes, in my limbs. Just lying here in bed, scarcely breathing, without making any physical exertion at all, is all I can do. I have a capacity for sleep like a blotter for ink.

I took health for granted, didn't I? Jesus, please be my healer.

The Mozart Sonata in B-flat Major for violin and piano is on the stereo. Otherwise, the room is silent.

I am in a moment of solitude. The sun and clouds through high windows make stark, fluid reflections on a white wall. An immense tree outside the window seems my nearest companion. It is older than I am and will outlive me.

I need to explore my inner world and do work there to liberate myself from the past.

Stay with me, Jesus, on my inner journey.

Why won't noon get here? Concentration seems to be my big problem today. Instead of concentrating, I'm allowing all kinds of thoughts and problems, big ones and small, to filter through. I need to make a list of priorities and follow it from top to bottom.

If I could just get out of here for a few minutes, take a walk, clear my head. I need to focus.

Suddenly, I realize I can sit right here and do that. I take a moment to center myself. The many competing, shouting voices inside me start to quiet down. I breathe consciously, knowingly, fill my lungs with air, release it slowly.

Equilibrium is restored. I can smile honestly at a certain awareness: As important as all this is, it isn't *that* important. What a difference it makes to know that.

I sit here stunned, Jesus. Out of the blue, without even a shade of warning, an impersonal phone call just changed the pattern of my life. It affected my work, place of living, relationships, and financial security.

I had taken everything for granted. My prospects appeared promising. In fact, it seemed I was clearly on a roll. Now my ego is so tamed that self-confidence has gone out the window.

What can I do? It seems you're telling me I must let go of defeatism and reach out to others for help. Life beckons to me as a member of the human race, neither a star nor a solitary player.

Thanks for taking hold of me when I need it most, Jesus.

My work makes me ask: What is effectiveness, Jesus? Some people place it ahead of honesty. But without honesty, wouldn't something just appear on the surface to be effective? It would really be a failure.

Success and failure seem to be badly misunderstood, don't they? They are judged by outward appearances instead of inner realities. I have felt deep failure at moments when people said I was a success. I have felt fulfilled and successful as a human being when I was most severely judged to be a failure.

You have taught us, Jesus, that a person can gain the whole world and lose one's soul. This seems to be true for whole nations and societies and business firms, too. Do we hear what you are saying?

I'm working late, Jesus. I decided to stay here, work my way through the stack of papers on my desk.

It's a luxurious feeling to be able to do this slowly, knowing I have plenty of time. My office phone won't ring. Mail won't come. A colleague won't stand at my door waiting to talk.

What an odd, not unwelcome, sensation to be alone here. It raises strange thoughts. For example, I realize the impersonal office isn't mine, although this is my second home eight hours a day. I look around at the pictures, books, and personal items I've brought in to create a sense of belonging. They'll be removed one day when I won't be here, either. However, in the moment at hand I feel secure and am gratefully alive.

The stack of papers that cluttered my desk has nearly disappeared, some into files, other pieces into a trash basket. The top of my desk is nearly clean.

I am doing the wash. The washer industriously whirs away while the dryer amiably tumbles a load. I pour detergent in the bottom to get the wash started and also clean the screen in the dryer. I place sheets in the bottom of the washer, with towels on top.

Then I sit down to read but can't concentrate because I know it will be necessary shortly to unload the dryer, transfer the finished wet laundry in the washer to the dryer, and place a new batch in the washer. I try to think of a short-range project to do in this limited amount of time, and fail.

Doing the wash isn't exactly a momentous feat. It won't get written up in the newspaper or make the six o'clock news, or even elicit particular comment. This seems grossly unfair. Doing the wash is far cleaner than lots of things going on today at City Hall, isn't it, Jesus?

I hear a man cry out in pain or anguish. I awaken suddenly—and realize I am coming out of a dream.

The man who cried out is a part of myself. He wishes to communicate, move from entombment inside myself, enter freely into my consciousness, come into my life.

He is a part of my inner life, which I have come to know in my dreams. I spend so much time and energy in my outer life, yet the inner one is compelling, real, holds answers to questions about meaning.

I am grateful for the call to wholeness in my dreams, Jesus; the challenging reality of my inner journey through the pilgrimage of life. Thanks for bringing together the lost fragments of my life, Jesus, calling me to truth and you.

I feel all alone in a traffic jam, Jesus. But I am not alone, of course. Several thousand other people are here, too. Yet I feel utterly solitary within the confines of my car.

Four lanes of the highway as far as my eyes can see are packed with cars unable to move. The standstill holds for miles ahead and behind. There is nothing I can do to change the situation.

At first I felt rage about my predicament. "Why is this happening again?" Then frustration. "I must get out of the city and move immediately to the country or a small town."

But now I begin to feel relaxed, almost euphoric. "It's rather nice not to be hurrying anywhere." I'm curiously reminded of when I had the measles as a kid and got to stay at home in bed instead of going to school. There was snow and ice outside, but inside my room it was warm and cozy.

Here on the crowded highway, trapped in what had seemed an antihuman situation, suddenly I feel human, Jesus. Humanity surrounds me, huddled in cars as I am. I know myself as a part of an immense adventure that is shared.

I ponder the meaning of my life. I know there is a face, a smile, and a frown. There is passion, a residue of rage, and an icy capacity to withdraw. There is the familiar body, the uncharted mind, and the chameleon performing as a clown.

I know there is a tenderness, a warmth, and sometimes a biting revenge that reacts to real or imaginary hurt. There is the man-woman, child, and the indelible image of God that calls to me in what I know as a conscience. There is a hunger that is insatiable, a thirst that burns and gnaws, and a hard selfishness that can be cruel.

I know there is a vaulting ambition, a drive that will not let me rest, and a laziness made for a summer's day. There is an idealism that can startle my self-interest, a sense of duty that can suffocate ticklish inclinations toward abandon, and a ruthless sense of self-sovereignty that can arrogantly try to bluff even almighty God.

I know there is a cultivated self-sufficiency, a core of loneliness, and a dreaded anxiety. There is a personal history with tears and laughter, a public life, and a being so vulnerable that it has been smashed into pieces like a glass.

What is there in me of holiness, Jesus? What is there within me possessing hidden life that cannot be broken or burned or obliterated? What is there of me that is love?

You became human, Jesus. You experienced loneliness, anger, joy, depression, and hope.

Thank you for becoming human like me, Jesus.

Death is somewhere up ahead, Jesus. Casting glances at me out of the corner of an eye, it waits for me.

But I'm not ready to leave the world's stage. Not yet. Let me play my roles in repertory, speak my lines, sing and dance. I want to read tomorrow morning's newspaper, answer a letter, make a fresh salad, meet a new friend, see a new film, and start a hot fire in the grate.

Let me live a while, I pray. Then, when death places its hand in mine, please stay with me, Jesus.

Dilemmas

I find it very difficult to pray in this situation. It seems to me we all have prayed a long time about situations like this yet have done little or nothing to change them. Maybe we thought prayer was magic, Jesus, and decided we didn't need to cooperate actively with you in working for a better world.

What are we to say about this family that lives in a wooden shack here on a winding dirt road? The family is hungry. As I see it, these persons have no opportunity to break out of the grinding, desperate life in which they have been prisoners since birth.

Lots of well-fed, comfortable, middle-class people everywhere are praying for "situations" like this all the time. But they don't seem to do enough about changing such situations by altering political and economic facts of life, or helping specific men, women, and children who are victims.

Isn't prayer expressed in action, Jesus, and isn't real action a form of prayer? Then maybe people in Chicago ought to pray for "situations" like this by getting involved in Chicago community organization efforts and in the lives of Chicago victims; perhaps people in Boston, London, São Paolo, and Johannesburg ought to pray in this way, too. And people in Mississippi, New York, Ohio, and Texas.

Or, if we do not intend to offer ourselves and cooperate with you in fighting evil—wouldn't it be more honest not to go through mere motions of praying, Jesus?

They're a black student and a white student, Jesus. The black student said, "I refuse to be a textbook for whites. I don't want a white roommate in the dorm. On my own time, I need to study or be with friends to relax. I'm not going to teach a white kid with my life."

The white student said, "I think what you're saying is racist. Get over playing the race card. There's nothing wrong with my being white. If my parents or grandparents hurt black people, that's not my problem."

Be with the black student and with the white student, Jesus, and help each to understand how the other feels. Where do all of us go from here—into one world or separate worlds?

I want to say thanks, Jesus. Anxiety had overtaken me. I'm surprised how faithless I was. Stress had set me up for a killing, I didn't ask you for help but tried to handle the crisis by myself and lost.

Everything blew up. When the smoke cleared I saw you standing there. I also saw how I had loused up my life by trying to play the majordomo.

I can't make it without you, Jesus. Thanks for starting over with me again.

I sit inside my jail, Jesus. I constructed it with my own hands, stone upon stone, lock inside lock. Here I am a model prisoner of my own will. Here I am the slave of self.

Freedom is what I long for, Jesus. My weary body and tired mind cry out for a new life. My soul is parched and life is in decay, with dreams crumbled and energy stifled. Depression is heavy upon me. I feel hopeless in this moment, Jesus. I am only sorry for myself. I ask if there is any use to struggle with life.

But still I want a voice to cut through my silence. Let me hear laughter. Let me see a burst of life.

I want to care again, Jesus.

This staff meeting is entirely too long. If Lucille, who has the floor, could relax and laugh and willingly give up some control, it would be easier for everybody. She has an apparent need to dominate and insist on her own way without compromise or give-and-take. It's troubling.

I look at Ben and can see he's on one of his roller-coaster mood swings. When Ben is up, dozens of new projects are dizzying in the air. When he's down, the brooding silence around him is an environment for a jungle war. This morning Ben is down.

Bad. Because everything seems on edge in the office so far today. Egos are unbearably twisted out of shape. Roger, ordinarily laid back, seems a veritable Niagara Falls, a supercharged workaholic, an obtrusive stranger who can't keep his mouth shut.

Looking around the room, I wonder how the others see *me* this morning. Do I look as preposterous as they do to me? My face breaks into a smile. I'm aware of how close I came to losing my sense of humor.

I realize this is a good community, filled with real people, essential to my life. I offer thanks for it.

I'm gripped and obsessed by envy of someone, Jesus. Is it because we're alike? Does that mean I hate a part of myself? The situation is embarrassing because, although I don't like to be with this person, we must work together.

I'm baffled by myself. It seems unlike me to be so irrational, arrogant, unloving, out of control. What's the matter with me?

Should I meet this person and confess my feelings? I realize that a strong hatred is filled with passion. Do I feel love for this person in ways I simply can't understand?

A great gulf is growing wider between us. I'm trapped by my pride. Help me, Jesus. Acid rain is falling.

I used to think I had forever to live. Life seemed to stretch out like an endless highway. There would be time for everything.

But when I found out today that Matt has AIDS, Jesus, I realized all of a sudden there's a real limit to life.

Not only Matt's. Mine too. Everybody's. Matt is a friend whom I love. I also love the world. It seems to me that in a real sense the world presently has AIDS. We need to heal it, all the people in it, and ourselves.

Maybe the best way, Jesus, is to love people, each other. Do you agree? Appreciate life and give thanks for it. Live each moment to the fullest. Be kind and generous. Offer warmth and nurturing in place of coldness and rejection. Identify evil within our hearts, and seek help to change it into goodness.

Wouldn't it be healing, Jesus, to breathe in honesty and breathe out joy? Help me to breathe that way, Jesus.

I believe that terror is evil, Jesus. Sometimes I am tempted to use it when I angrily protest against the terrorism of the status quo. An eye for an eye. A tooth for a tooth. Injustice for injustice. A life for a life.

But if one became a tyrant to defeat a tyrant, wouldn't that already mean defeat? One would have become one's enemy, and corrupted.

Murder doesn't win people's hearts. Burning, exploding, and destroying don't make people love. Some people think it is soft to love. I don't think so, Jesus. Do you?

I see a cockroach. I'd rather see a martian standing in my home today. Does this mean there's a horde of roaches waiting in the wings like Attila the Hun and his followers? Or is this a sole cockroach—a courageous innovator, a wiry loner?

Am I compelled to kill this afternoon, or may I be magnanimous?

Who, I wonder, decides what creatures are accepted as a part of life, and what creatures aren't? Sometimes humans find themselves in the same position. I look at the cockroach; it looks at me. Clearly, it's a very specific form of creation, as I am. It appears to be intricate, complex, and mysterious.

At least for today, I make a decision to place cockroach rights ahead of the status quo. Can't God's creatures appreciate one another?

He's gossiping again about other people who work here. I can always tell when Brian gets that glint in his eyes, walks into my office, and shuts the door. Then he starts to dish about someone in particular or nearly everybody in general. I can imagine what he says about me behind my back.

It depresses me and drains my energy to hear him spew out his apparent dislike of other people here. Afterward, when my eyes meet *theirs,* I feel guilty that I even heard all the lies and fantasies about them.

I've told Brian several times not to share his gossip with me, but it does no good; he seems not to hear. Gossip is to him what booze is to an alcoholic.

He opens all the available sewers to let his germs spread. The danger is that he spreads his distorted, hateful, envious views of others. So, Brian's views take on a life of their own. He gives them life.

When he ridicules and cuts people to ribbons, Jesus, I try to combat him by seeing the people in their fantastic human beauty and wholeness.

Clark started to shout at me. He had come into my office, closed the door, and angrily confronted me. I was absolutely surprised. His face got red and he talked so rapidly he didn't stop to take a breath.

Clark has long been my closest work friend. On various occasions he has drifted into my office to share the most intimate life details, yearnings, plans, opinions.

But today he seemed vicious in things he said. We had never fought before, and he had never indicated any hostility toward me. Abruptly, he fell silent and sat down. In a moment he held his head in his hands and cried.

His marriage, he explained, seemed to be on the rocks. Although he's been under extraordinary stress for several weeks, he felt unable to share his feelings about it before this morning.

Simple communication between people is such a mystery to me, Jesus. When Clark stood there, enraged and shouting at me, it had nothing to do with me at all. Help me to remember this, Jesus. Help me to remember this.

It's a strange party, Jesus. The people seem to be tense. They are in constant motion and play tight roles, scripted and choreographed.

A woman dressed in gold pajamas and enough costume jewelry to sink an excursion boat has apparently had too much to drink. She keeps saying: "I want to work with the poor in Africa. . . . the poor . . . Africa . . . I want to work with the poor in Africa."

I wonder, Jesus, what she really wants and what is her Africa.

In the City

It's a jazz spot, Jesus. He's a musician who works here. Jazz for him is art and life. This is the way he expresses himself, tells it as it is, hangs on, and climbs.

But the nightclub world is a tough one if you want to be free and be yourself. It's interested in top stars and pop performers. Steady work and the buck go together, and both are somewhat elusive. At least, that's his experience.

It's late in here tonight, Jesus. The customers are listening over their drinks; they're getting scared because soon they'll have to go into the dark night outside. There won't be any music or Scotch or lights out there on the early-morning streets. If there was someplace to go, they'd leave, but this is the last place open.

The musician is wondering if they're hearing him at all through their listening. He has something to say, and he's saying it. It's about death and life, sex and hunger, knowing yourself and being known, the dream, the vision. He's looking at the people, right into their dead and alive eyes, and he wants them to hear him.

Does he know you hear him, Jesus?

Look up at that window where the old guy is sitting. See, he's half-hidden by the curtain that's moving a little in the breeze. That tenement—it's a poor place to have to live, isn't it, Jesus?

He is seated alone at a kitchen table and looking blankly out the window. He lives with his sister, who is away working all day. There is nothing for him to do. He doesn't have any money; all he has is time.

Who is he in my life, Jesus? What has he got to do with me? He's your brother, and you love him. What does this say to me, Christ? I don't know what sense I am supposed to make out of this. I mean, how can I possibly be responsible in any honest, meaningful way for that guy?

He just moved a short bit away from the window. Maybe he moved because he felt my eyes on him from the sidewalk down here. I didn't mean to embarrass him; I just wanted to let him know somebody understands he's alive and he's your brother, so he's not alone or lost. Does he know it, Jesus?

The kids are smiling, Jesus, on the tenement stoop. The little girl is the oldest, and she's apparently in charge of the younger two, her brothers.

But suddenly she's crying and her two brothers are trying to comfort her. Now everything seems to be peaceful, and she's smiling again.

But what's ahead for them, Christ? Home is this broken-down dump on a heartless, tough street. What kind of school will they go to? Will it be hopelessly overcrowded? Will it be a place that breeds despair? Will it change these kids' happy smiles into angry, sullen masks they'll have to wear for the rest of their lives?

I look at their faces and realize how they are our victims, especially when we like to say they are beautiful children, but we don't change conditions that will make their faces hard and their hearts cynical.

Have these kids got a chance, Jesus? Will they know anything about dignity or love or health? Jesus, looking at these kids, I'm afraid for them and for all of us.

The old house is nearly all torn down, Jesus. What became of the people who used to live here? Where are they now, and what has happened to the roots they had here?

The demolition men are doing a good job. A week ago they started cold, and now the house is just about down. I saw them taking it down floor by floor, room by room. They tied a rope onto the wooden frames of rooms and pulled them, bringing them tumbling down onto the ground. Suddenly the derelict old house is nearly gone. In a day or so there will be only a patch of ground on a city block where people made love, men and women fought and relaxed and worked, babies were born, and death visited from time to time. It will be strange for people who used to live here when they come back home and there isn't any home.

Help us to learn how to live with mobility and rapid change and the absence of old securities, remembering that you didn't have any place to lay your head when you lived among us.

This is a gay bar, Jesus. It looks like any other bar on the outside, only it isn't. Men stand three and four deep at this bar—some just feeling a sense of belonging here, others making contacts for new partners.

This isn't very much like a church, Christ, but many members of the church are also here in this bar. Quite a few of the men here belong to the church as well as to this bar. If they knew how, a number of them would ask you to be with them in both places. Some of them wouldn't, but won't you be with them, too, Jesus?

She's probably the most popular girl in high school.
She's certainly one of the best looking, and she has a
very real smile and seems completely secure, Jesus. You
could hardly find anyone who dislikes her.

But she dislikes herself, or, at least, the self she feels
she was handed but can't figure out. She thinks she must
be two different selves, the operating one and another
that is hidden under layers of complexity she can't get
to. She wants to find out who that other self is because
she believes she would like to be it. She simply doesn't
know the self everybody seems to be relating to.

Everybody responds to her smile. She is tired of it
and has come to feel it's a lie of some kind. She wants
friends who would like that *other* self instead of this
one which is a stranger—or enemy—to her.

The other night she broke up with the boy she
likes. She cared too much about him to let him be hurt.
She thought she should find out who she is before she
lets anybody she cares about get too involved with *this*
self. She wanted to love him with her other self but
didn't know how or who that self might be.

Here she comes now, Jesus, smiling her way across
the campus. Help me to smile back—at her *other* self.

He doesn't know how his children are going to eat tonight, Jesus. There is just no money left. He has tried everything but cannot find a job. His wife is sick and doesn't have the right kind of care.

His little girl is crying. The sound of it is a bit louder than the dialogue of an old movie that is playing on the TV set. His boys are sitting huddled on an old sofa watching the images flicker on the television screen.

Jesus, he wishes that he knew what to do.

They're in a golden world, Jesus. They're having a party in a hotel suite, which is elegant and located in the best hotel in the heart of the city. There's music, jewelry, glamour, gin, VIP status, and POWER.

But nobody's having any fun. They're too busy sparring with one another in the POWER game, which, tonight, is also the sex-and-booze tournament.

Everybody looks slick and, underneath tans and wigs, somewhat lonely. They're only observing the stiff protocol of small talk and ground rules. This informal gathering is as rigid as the court of Louis XIV, only the accents here are of Detroit, Houston, and Los Angeles.

The masks are on parade tonight, Jesus. The masks are smiling and laughing to cover up status anxieties and bleeding ulcers.

Tell us about freedom, Jesus.

Prayers without Words

David says he prays without being aware of it when he paints, Jesus. He says this is the real link that keeps him creating and able to function as an artist.

Is this true? Can David's painting be praying? If so, is it possible Richard prays in his social work studies, and Ruth when she edits her magazine, Bob while he types letters, and Estelle when she cleans people's apartments?

Help me to pray that way, too. I want to pray in my doing and being, Jesus.

Daniel stands by the grave, wanting to pray, not knowing any words. He is forty years old, an intellectual and cultural figure in the city. Many years ago, Daniel relinquished his religious background and community. He didn't look back and never felt a sense of loss.

Daniel married and became the father of a son eight years ago. The boy grew and thrived and was a source of enormous joy and pride to Daniel. But a few days ago his son was killed in an automobile accident.

Daniel stands at the young boy's fresh grave. He feels a compelling impulse to *do* something besides just stand here. It occurs to him to say a simple prayer—perhaps for his son, or somehow about the entire situation surrounding his sudden and untimely death, with its resulting pain and confusion. Yet Daniel realizes he does not know the words of a single prayer.

His desire is to pray. His intention is to pray. Slowly, it dawns on him that he is expressing, "saying," incarnating a prayer, by being here.

Nancy is a teacher. Friends wonder why she's willing to work so hard for so little, to make this kind of a commitment in a world that often seems disinterested in unselfish giving.

Nancy sticks it out—the human and motivational problems she faces in the classroom, bureaucratic red tape in the education system, the long distances she travels to work in a poverty area where she believes there is a special need.

How to teach students who are hungry and tired and disillusioned. How to interest them in ideas and challenges that may give them an opportunity to break out of an iron ring of deprivation and unequal opportunity.

Nancy stands at a blackboard, chalk in hand, talking and gesturing.

Our marching had a rhythm. About twenty of us had been marching in the snow, in a constant circular movement in front of an apartment house, for nearly three hours.

The time: 1961. The place: the inner city of Detroit. We carried signs reading, "Negroes Can't Live Here," "We Oppose Discrimination," "End Segregated Housing," and "Freedom."

We marched because a woman we knew had been denied housing in the apartment building because she was black.

It grew colder. Snow was falling quickly now, blanketing the sidewalk. The wind blew snow into our eyes. I removed my gloves and dug bare hands deep inside my overcoat pockets, flexing them to restore circulation.

"Why can't people live where they want to?" a man angrily asked. That was, we felt, the point of our demonstration. People flashed glances from passing cars: quizzical, hating, noncommittal, friendly, bored.

Our picketing continued in the afternoons for four weeks until the black woman moved into the apartment house.

She has ten million dollars. Barbara won't be awake this morning when her maid arrives for work. In fact, the worst moment in her day is the first one upon awakening. She faces a gnawing emptiness.

It isn't that she has nothing to do. She is on a dozen symphony and art museum committees for big donors, and is a main contributor to a posh church that she attends without fail once each year on Easter morning. Daily she lunches at the country club or any restaurant of her choice. She can fly on an instant's notice to San Francisco, London, or Sydney.

Yet all the therapy in the world hasn't given her a motivating reason to face another day. A pragmatist, Barbara got off liquor a long time ago and resolutely stayed off it. Boredom is the enemy. Her husband walks through his own paces, which meet hers in the midst of yet another social gathering. Her children, away at school, are strangers who smile handsomely when they hold out their hands for more money.

God, she wishes that something mattered.

Joe is getting drunk again. He doesn't drink the hard stuff anymore, only beer and wine, but that's lethal brew for him. He's naked, seated at the kitchen table. And alone. Susan, his wife, left last week for what she said would be the last time.

Joe's driver's license had long permitted him simply to drive from home to work and back. He violated that agreement many times and ten days ago was the cause of a traffic accident. He has no license now. He was fired from his job for lousing it up, this following a period of probation, which he broke by continuing to drink.

He has a six-pack on the floor and a gallon of cheap wine open on the kitchen table. Joe pours another tumbler of warm, sweet, white wine.

His mind moves back over the years to a happy marriage, a good job, a promising career, friends too numerous to count on the fingers of both hands.

Right now, he is without any of these. There is nowhere to go, no phone calls to place, no hope of anything new in his life. Joe sits in the chair and looks at a blank wall. His open hands ask.

For nine years, Ken was a dialysis patient, kept alive by a kidney machine. "I've had hundreds of transfusions," he said. "I received four pints of blood every three weeks during that time. A shunt was put in my arm—a plastic hose attached to an artery and a vein deep in my arm."

When he had a mysterious bout with high blood pressure, the medical decision was made that a transplant was necessary. The wait began for a good kidney match. It was found.

"What did all this mean? Would the transplant work? Who had died that I might live and have a better chance at life? I remember that things got hazy with shots, surgery lights, and an unpleasant gadget in my throat."

The transplant was successful, but there was no certainty it might not be rejected after one month, one year, or five years of good functioning. "One of the things about having a terminal disease is that I find I can be intellectually honest and not play games," he explains.

Ken laughs easily and gently, greeting a doctor who has just come in to see how he is doing. Trying to go on living is his prayer.

Pam is a volunteer twice a week in a city shelter for homeless people. She also holds down a job and lives with her two young children, whose support she provides, and her mother. Pam discovers excitement in dozens of small challenges and events that make up her days. Hope, not a mere word for her, is translated into serving others.

After watching her grandmother slowly die in a county nursing home, Pam is grateful she can take care of her mother. She delights in her children and thanks God she has strength to provide for their needs.

Pam rides to work on a bus. Today is nasty, drizzling and cold, outside the bus window through which she looks. But Pam is animated and happy. Her service to others is Pam's prayer.

Jesus Prayers

Why is reality about you shocking to us, Jesus? They've made the cross you hung on so pretty.

I know the real cross wasn't pretty at all. But I guess I understand why they want to make copies of it out of fine woods and even semiprecious stones, because *you* hung on it.

Yet doesn't this romanticize your death and give it a kind of gloss it didn't have? Your death was bloody and dirty and very real. Can't we face it that way, Jesus? And can't we face the fact that you were a real human being, living a human life, as well as God?

Help us to understand, Jesus, your pain and your prayer. On the cross, when you asked why God had forsaken you, what did it really mean?

Were you reciting an old psalm or were you actually conscious of seemingly having been forgotten by God in a terribly painful and lost moment of time?

People have said this moment represented the depth of your agony on the cross, a spiritual crucifixion within the physical crucifixion. They have said your mental anguish was fused here with your bodily torture.

Yet you cried out to God. You never felt totally cut off from God. To me this has always seemed your deepest prayer.

Help me to know what you meant here, Christ.

Thanks for what you did about success and failure. Jesus, you ruined all the phony success stories forever when you didn't come down from the cross, turn your crown of thorns into solid gold, transform the crowd at Golgotha into a mighty army, march on Rome, and become *the king.*

Now all our success symbols in an age of global celebrity and consumerism look so shoddy and ephemeral over against your cross. You redefined forever the true meaning of authentic success. You revealed that what the world mockingly calls failure may be ennobled as sacrifice and service.

Thank you for refusing to play the stereotype role of the ultimate big shot.

Do you need me to act as your public relations person, Jesus? I don't think you do. I may work in your service, but your success doesn't depend upon my success. You do not fail if I am not effective. This frees me from a terrible slavery to myself under the guise of succeeding for you.

You are not mocked. Your reign has already come. It is established in human life. I can cooperate with it but never usher it in.

Why do some people say it is necessary to win money, large numbers of converts, publicity, and prestige for you? It has led to the church's fatal silence on issues where following you would have meant its own loss of these things.

Some Christians speak of the church as an army. You are presumably the general, Jesus, and the army is supposed to fight valiantly for your victory in the world, even if it must sometimes kill, maim, or pillage.

Is anyone, anywhere, ever meant to be manipulated, sacrificed, or dehumanized for your success, Jesus?

Help us really to dig in, Jesus, and be with you. After all the poor fiction and cheap biblical movies that have turned your life and death into almost bizarre superstition, Jesus, it's hard for me to see your cross as it really was.

They've even turned Jerusalem into such a tourist attraction that it's not at all easy, even when walking along the actual ground you walked, to visualize anything with honesty or accuracy.

I imagine it was sweaty and hot. When you said from the cross, "I thirst," I am sure you were very thirsty. It's easy for us today to say you were really thirsting for people's souls (and I'm sure you were), but isn't this just a dodge that keeps us from accepting the fact of your humanity? Why do we want to forget that you were human, hanging on the cross for hours, needing something to drink?

Can we somehow get through all the decoration that has been developed about the cross and just be quiet and be there with you?

A prayer of discipleship: "Send me." But where? To do what?

To bring pardon where there had been injury in a life I casually brushed against at my daily work? (But I had thought of mediating a teenage gang war in Chicago!)

To help turn doubt into faith in a person with whom I live intimately in my circle of family or friends? (But I had thought of helping a tired drunk from skid row!)

"Send me." Send me next door, into the next room, to speak somehow to a human heart beating alongside mine. Send me to bear a note of dignity into a subhuman situation. Send me to show forth joy in a moment and a place where there is otherwise no joy but only the will to die.

Send me to reflect your light in the darkness of futility, mere existence, and the horror of casual human cruelty. But give me your light, too, Jesus, in my own darkness and need.

Jesus: Take fire and burn away our guilt and our lying hypocrisies.

Take water and wash away our brothers' and sisters' blood, which we have caused to be shed.

Take hot sunlight and dry the tears of those we have hurt, and heal their wounded souls, minds, and bodies.

Take love and root it in our hearts, so that community may grow, transforming the dry desert of our prejudices and hatreds.

Take our imperfect prayers and purify them, so that we mean what we pray and are prepared to give ourselves to you along with our words.

Afterword

by Frederick H. Borsch,
Episcopal Bishop of Los Angeles

Prayer is, above all, presence. Prayer is awareness of the presence of the Divine Awareness—the Spirit of all life—as the context for our lives. Our prayer is then being present with and to this Spirit. It is making ourselves available. At its best, it is being available as one would with someone who is close and intimate.

In his prayers, Malcolm Boyd, a companion in spiritual struggles and on faith's pilgrimage, finds this presence and friendship in Jesus. He chooses Jesus because he believes Jesus has chosen him as Jesus has chosen all of us. Jesus has done so by being the One in whom the Spirit of life has known and shared fully in all it means to be human.

Malcolm tells of his discovery, now a number of years ago, that the Spirit of Jesus is not some distant God whom one must try to address in formal language. Rather, Jesus is here and present. Malcolm can speak with Jesus because he trusts that Jesus already knows about human pain and laughter, our bewilderment and our hope.

There is, therefore, nothing to hide. The prayers pour out with candor and spontaneity. They can use the language of everyday life, just as do many of Jesus' stories in the Bible. Sometimes that freshness will be eloquent. Sometimes, Malcolm tells us, he must struggle to find words for his hurts and his limping faith, his awe and passions and misplaced pride. He can then feel the Spirit of Jesus moving within him with, as Saint Paul put it, "sighs too deep for words." But, then, because we must still reach for some expression of our fears and longing, words tumble out.

When we pray with such honesty and openness, we are, in a sense, many selves. Malcolm tells Jesus of his many selves and moods. With Jesus, he can be quirky and caring. He can know himself as kind and unkind, loving and lonely, scared and impatient, while sometimes surprised by contentment and some of life's smallest pleasures. Compassion often rises in his prayers as he sees someone sick with AIDS, tortured by drugs, worn-out from farm labor, or having lost his beloved eight-year-old son. He turns to Jesus and prays to him in his suffering on the cross and feels Jesus' compassion and suffering in his prayers.

Nor are we spared as we are drawn with these prayers into what is in many ways an autobiography. I am reminded of what Frederick Buechner once said about some of the best-known theologians. They "are all telling us the stories of their lives, and if you press them far enough, even at their most cerebral and forbidding, you find an experience of flesh and blood, a human face smiling or frowning or weeping or covering its eyes before something that happened once."

So does Malcolm share with us in these prayers, which have been written over a number of years. One senses his own movement toward a more reflective perspective on life with Jesus. Although he is still running, because, I suppose, life and time are running, too, there is a deep watching and listening as well. One hears it in the description of the old house being torn down, when Malcolm prays: "Help us to learn how to live with mobility and change and the absence of old securities, remembering that you didn't have any place to lay your head when you lived among us." I hear in that prayer a resonance with an insight of Robert

Frost, who wrote about the gift of swiftness in terms of the power of standing still.

Malcolm's office is the world of his observations and prayers, but he also has an office in our Cathedral Center, a place of worship, hospitality, and servant ministry. Here Malcolm thinks and prays and writes. From here he offers courses to others who would learn more about poetry, prayer, and writing. To this office come the wondering and friends to share some of their thoughts, their concerns, and their yearning for company along the way. I am glad to be one of them.

Afterword

by Rev. Paul Wennes Egertson, Ph.D.,
Bishop, Southern California West Synod,
Evangelical Lutheran Church in America

The year I was born in North Dakota, Malcolm Boyd was winning awards for writing at his junior high school in Colorado. How strange that our paths should cross on the back nine of our lives. Having a hand in this publication of his prayers and meditations is deeply satisfying to me. For, unknown to him, his writings have brought gospel to me at critical forks along the road of my life and ministry.

When some of these prayers were first published in the runaway bestseller, *Are You Running with Me, Jesus?* I was serving a congregation in Las Vegas, Nevada, and trying to develop a ministry to the entertainers and tourists on the Las Vegas Strip. Given my own religious history, it was an unlikely effort. Born in the Midwest and raised in a parsonage observant of Norwegian Lutheran piety, I was prone to urge *absence* from places like the Las Vegas Strip rather than any sort of *presence*.

But there were those pesky stories of Jesus in the gospel texts assigned for preaching on Sundays. They made me wonder where *he* would be present if his ministry had been in the deserts of Nevada rather than Palestine. I couldn't escape the question, Where are the "tax collectors and sinners" in *this* community? It was known, after all, as Sin City!

The more I resisted the obvious answer to that question, the more I came to see myself as the elder brother in the field or one of those Pharisees and scribes whom Luke reports grumbling, "This fellow welcomes sinners and eats with them." The question then became, Am I running with you, Jesus?

God's timing is as amazing as God's grace. Just when I was undergoing a reluctant repentance for my righteousness, Malcolm's prayers arrived. The *worldliness* of their content and style helped me understand the longings running deep in the hearts of those to whom I now was called.

But sharing the gospel with people who didn't speak the language of Zion meant that I had to speak in tongues unknown to me. *Are You Running with Me, Jesus?* was my first primer in the grammar of worldly gospel speech. It was a concrete instance of Bonhoeffer's more abstract concept of worldly Christianity.

During those turbulent '60s, experimental ministries were going on all over the country. Coffeehouses were an emerging model. They were really nonalcoholic nightclubs. As I struggled with the lure of trying that approach in the Las Vegas milieu, the media reported that an Episcopal priest was booked into the hungry i in San Francisco. Here was my mentor in worldly Christianity again, now reciting his prayers and meditations in a real nightclub, sharing a stage with the comedian and social protester Dick Gregory. Was this ministerial heresy or creativity? Or was it simply running with Jesus? Whatever others thought, for me it was a sign pointing the way into the world.

A dozen years later, in 1978, one of my sons came out to his mother and me. Here was another call to enter a reality of which we were profoundly unaware and for which we lacked even a basic vocabulary. The story is too long to tell here but is available elsewhere.[1] Suffice it to say, resources on that subject

1. See "One Family's Story," in *Homosexuality and Christian Faith*, ed. Walter Wink (Minneapolis: Fortress Press, 1999), 23–30.

from Christian writers at that time were stunningly few and pathetically uninformed.

But what did I find? That very same year another missal arrived from my mentor in worldly Christianity. His book *Take Off the Masks* was Malcolm's act of "taking a lantern and casting bright light into what was a forbidden dungeon of my life." By courageously doing so, he also lit up a forbidden dungeon in the church's life. He played a key role in initiating the next major transformation of social consciousness to follow the struggles over racism and sexism. Such is the power of honest witness through the ministry of writing.

Twenty years after that, in 1998, we were planning our annual Bishop's Colloquy, a two-day gathering of all rostered ministers in our synod. At lunch one day, Bishop Frederick Borsch mentioned that Malcolm was the Poet/Writer in Residence at the Los Angeles Cathedral Center of St. Paul. I immediately invited him to come and share his journey with Jesus at our colloquy. It was there that I met him for the first time.

Again, the timing was amazing. A storm came through Santa Barbara that day, knocking out all the electricity. That evening, 120 clergy sat around tables lit by candles, while Malcolm stood at a podium lit by a flashlight, bearing witness to his run with Jesus. It was a magical night. Was it the hungry i all over again? For the first time I heard orally what I had only seen printed before. Then I knew why Luther insisted on the supremacy of the living voice over the printed page. Hearing these prayers spoken helped me understand why they were so powerful, even in print.

In one of James Montgomery's hymns, we sing:

> Prayer is the soul's sincere desire,
> Uttered or unexpressed,
> The motion of a hidden fire
> That trembles in the breast.

The church has a rich treasury of uttered prayer, much of which is contained in the *Book of Common Prayer,* where Malcolm's spiritual life was tutored. But it speaks the language of Zion, deeply meaningful only to those who are living in Zion. What Malcolm's prayers do is give utterance to the sincere desire that is unexpressed but burning in the breasts of people in the world who do not know their trembling is praying in tongues. Malcolm has the spiritual gift of interpretation.

Now, out of that candlelit night, these prayers and meditations come into print once more. I thank God, and then Malcolm, for what his ministry through writing has meant to me and mine. But let me suggest to the reader that their power will be fully released when you go back and read them aloud.